Internet links

If you have access to the Internet, you can visit the websites we have recommended in this book. If you don't have use of the Internet, don't worry. This book is a complete, fun and interesting book on its own.

Usborne Quicklinks

For links to all the websites, go to the **Usborne Quicklinks Website** at **www.usborne-quicklinks.com** and type in the keywords "pocket tigers". There you'll find links that you can click on to take you straight to the recommended websites. The links are regularly checked, reviewed and updated. If any of the sites close down we will, if possible, replace them with suitable alternatives.

Downloadable pictures

Pictures in this book with the symbol ✍ can be downloaded from Usborne Quicklinks free of charge for your own personal use, for example on a greeting card to a friend. The pictures may not be used ~~~~~~~~~~~~

Internet safety

When using the Internet, please make sure you follow these guidelines:
• Ask your parent's or guardian's permission before you connect to the Internet.
• If you write a message in a website guest book or on a website message board, do not include any personal information such as your full name or email address.
• If a website asks you to log in or register by typing your name or email address, ask permission of an adult first.
• If you receive an email from someone you don't know, tell an adult and do not reply to the email.
• Never arrange to meet anyone you have met on the Internet.

We recommend that children are supervised while on the Internet, that they do not use Internet chat rooms, and that you use Internet filtering software to block unsuitable material. For more information, see inside the back cover.

Why do Tigers have Stripes?

INTERNET - LINKED

Why do Tigers have Stripes?

Mike Unwin

Designed by Sharon Bennet
Illustrated by Robert Morton, Steven Kirk, Gillian Miller,
Robert Gillmor, Treve Tamblin and Stuart Trotter
Edited by Helen Edom and revised by Philippa Wingate
Cover design by Russell Punter
Cover illustration by Christyan Fox
With thanks to Non Figg and Katarina Dragoslavić
Consultant: Dr. Margaret Rostron

CONTENTS

A world of colours

Many animals, such as tigers, have interesting colours or patterns. This book explains how colours and patterns help all kinds of animals from the fiercest tigers to the most helpless insects.

A tiger has a striped pattern. Can you think of any other animals with stripes?

Matching colours

Different animals' colours often match the places where they live. The oryx is an antelope that lives in the desert. Its pale colour matches the sandy background.

In deserts there are few places to hide from enemies. Sandy animals are hard to spot because they blend in. Colours or patterns that help animals to hide are called camouflage.

Some desert animals live in holes. When they come out their sandy-coloured camouflage helps them hide from hunters such as hawks and foxes.

An oryx is pale like the desert.

Scorpion

Gerbil

Hidden hunters

Most animals run away if they see a hunter coming. Camouflage helps hunters to hide so they can catch other animals to eat.

Snowy owls live in the Arctic where there is lots of snow. They hunt small creatures called lemmings. The owls' white feathers match the snow. It is hard for lemmings to spot them.

Lemmings

White feathers blend in with the snow and sky

Forest greens

Many animals that live in rainforests are green to match the colours of the leaves. This camouflage makes them very hard to see.

Look at the green tree frog in this picture. How many other animals can you spot?

Tree frog

Blue waters

Camouflage is also important under the sea. Many sharks and other fish are blue or grey to blend in with the colours underwater.

Blue sharks

For a link to a website with shark videos, go to www.usborne-quicklinks.com

Patterns

Background colours are not the only kind of camouflage. Patterns also help animals to hide.

Breaking up shapes

A tiger in the zoo looks big, bright and easy to see. But in the forests and long grass where it hunts, a tiger can be hard to see. A tiger's stripes seem to break up its shape into small pieces. It is hard to see among the patterns and shadows of the background. This helps it to creep up on animals.

Seeing in black and white

This black and white picture shows how a leopard looks to an antelope.

Many animals such as antelope cannot see colours. They see in black and white. This makes it very hard for them to make out an animal, such as a leopard, whose pattern breaks up its shape.

Lying in wait

The gaboon viper is a snake that lives on the ground in African forests. Its complicated pattern makes its shape hard to see against the leaves.

Small animals cannot see a gaboon viper lying in wait for them. When they get close, the viper kills them with a bite from its poisonous fangs.

From a distance

The ringed plover lives on beaches. Close up its markings look bright. But from a distance you can only see a pattern that looks like the pebbles.

If the plover keeps still, it seems to disappear into the stony background. Enemies cannot spot it unless they are close.

Ringed plover

Seaweed shapes

The sargassum fish has strange lumps of skin that stick out from its body. These make its shape hard to see. It seems to disappear among the seaweed where it lives.

People hiding

Soldiers wear uniforms with special patterns. This helps them to blend into the background, just like tigers do.

For a link to a website which shows how animals blend in with their surroundings, go to www.usborne-quicklinks.com

Shadows and light

For a link to a website with fun facts and an online game about animals and camouflage, go to www.usborne-quicklinks.com

Light and shadows can make animals stand out from their background.

Lying flat

This bird is called a stone curlew. It is well camouflaged but you can still see its shadow. In the daylight, solid things always have shadows. This helps you to see where they are.

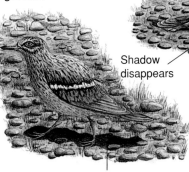

Shadow disappears

Stone curlew's shadow

A stone curlew lies flat on the ground so it looks small. This makes its shadow disappear so it is even harder for enemies to spot.

Flat shapes

Some animals have flattened bodies. Enemies do not notice them because they leave hardly any shadow.

Flaps of skin on a gecko's tail make it look flat.

The flying gecko is a lizard that lives on tree trunks. It has a flat body with flaps of skin that press down on the bark. This helps it to hide.

Dark and pale

You can often spot solid things by seeing the light shining on them.

Sunlight makes the top of this rock look lighter than the background.

No sunlight reaches the bottom, so it looks darker than the background.

The impala, like many animals, is coloured dark above and pale below. This is the opposite of the natural light and shadow that fall on its body. It makes the impala harder to pick out from its background.

From below

Many water birds such as puffins are white underneath. They swim on the surface of the water and dive down to catch fish.

From underwater the surface looks bright because of sunlight above it. It is hard for fish to spot puffins from below. Their white undersides are hidden against the bright surface of the water.

Hiding with mirrors

Many sea fish, such as shad, have shiny silver scales on their sides and bellies. Underwater these scales work like mirrors. They reflect the colour of the water, so the fish become almost invisible.

7

Disguises

Some animals are shaped to look like other things. This helps them to hide. These insects all have disguises that help them hide in forests.

This caterpillar looks just like a bird dropping, so nothing wants to eat it.

The thorn bug looks just like a thorn on a branch.

The leaf butterfly's folded wings look like a leaf on the forest floor.

The stick insect looks just like twigs.

Standing straight

Animals can help their disguises to work by the way they behave. The tawny frogmouth is a bird with colours like bark. If it is in danger, it points its beak upwards so it looks like a dead branch.

Deadly flowers

The flower mantis is a hunting insect. Its body is the same colour and shape as the flowers where it hides.

Other insects that visit the flower do not notice the mantis lying in wait to catch them.

Like a log

A crocodile in the water can look just like a floating log. This disguise helps it to catch antelope that come to the water to drink.

The crocodile's rough skin looks like old tree bark.

Dressing up

Some animals disguise themselves by decorating their bodies. The sponge crab lives on the sea bed. It holds a sponge on its back legs.

This helps the crab to look like part of the sea bed.

Antelope don't notice the crocodile. When it gets close, it grabs an antelope with its huge jaws and pulls it into the water.

For a link to a website about crocodiles, go to *www.usborne-quicklinks.com*

Surprises

Some animals stop enemies attacking by tricking or surprising them. They often use colours or patterns to help.

Frightening eyes

Many hunters are frightened if they suddenly see a big pair of eyes.

This swallowtail caterpillar has patterns that look like eyes. Birds think they belong to a bigger, more dangerous creature, so they leave the caterpillar alone.

The caterpillar's real eyes are hidden underneath.

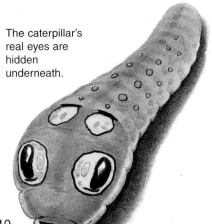

A bright flash

Bark

The red underwing moth looks well camouflaged on bark. But if it is spotted by a bird, it opens its top wings to show the bright red underneath.

A sudden flash of red surprises the bird. It leaves the moth alone.

Missing the target

This hairstreak butterfly has a pattern on its wings that looks like another head. Birds peck at the wings by mistake. This gives the butterfly time to escape.

Head pattern

The real head is at this end.

Puffing up

Some animals make
themselves look bigger
to trick enemies. A
long-eared owl spreads
its wings and puffs up
its feathers to frighten
enemies away.

This owl looks twice
as big as usual.

Playing dead

Some hunters, such as hawks, only
attack living creatures. An opossum
is a small animal that pretends to be
dead when it is in danger. When the
danger has gone, the opossum gets
up again.

An opossum
pretends to be
dead by rolling
over with its
mouth open.

Looking both ways

In India tigers sometimes attack
farmers. Tigers are scared by
people's faces so they
attack from behind.
Farmers wear masks
on the backs of their
heads to scare
tigers away.

Keep-away colours

Some animals do not try to hide. They have bright colours and patterns that are meant to be seen. These colours are a warning to their enemies.

Remembering colours

Black and yellow patterns are easy for animals to remember. Wasps are bright yellow and black. They can give their enemies a painful sting.

Black and yellow are warning colours.

If a young bird is stung by a wasp, it remembers its pattern. It will not try to catch a wasp again, because it knows that black and yellow things hurt.

Eating bees

A few birds, such as bee-eaters, have found a way to eat bees safely. They are not put off by warning colours. Bee-eaters strike a bee against a branch so its sting is squeezed out and broken.

Being seen

Many poisonous animals do not run away. Instead they show off their warning colours to their enemies.

The deadly poisonous arrow-poison frog does not hop away from enemies like other frogs do. It crawls around slowly so it can easily be seen.

*For a link to a website with an online activity where you can see how animals use their camouflage to hide from predators and prey, go to **www.usborne-quicklinks.com***

Fierce black and white

The ratel is an African badger. Its white back makes it easy to see. Although it is quite small, it is very fierce and is not afraid of any other animal.

The ratel has strong teeth and claws.

The ratel does not need to keep a look-out for danger like most animals do. Its colours warn enemies that it is too dangerous to attack.

Smelly warning

Skunks are small animals with a bold pattern. They can squirt a nasty, smelly liquid at enemies such as dogs.

A spotted skunk stands up on its front legs to show its pattern. This warns the dog to stay back. If the dog comes closer, the skunk sprays it.

Signals for people
People use warning colour just like animals do. Red often means "hot", "stop" or "danger".

This red tap warns you to be careful because the water is hot.

13

Copying colours

Some animals survive because they have colours and patterns that help them to look like other kinds of animals.

Poisonous or safe

Can you tell the difference between these two snakes? The coral snake is very poisonous. Its bright colours are a warning.

Coral snake

The king snake looks like a coral snake, but it is not poisonous at all. If you look hard you can see its pattern is slightly different.

King snake

Other animals are afraid to attack the king snake because it looks like a poisonous coral snake.

Which is the wasp?

Some insects look just like wasps, even though they do not really have stings. Most animals do not attack these insects because their colours remind them of stinging wasps.

Can you guess which insect is a wasp? Look on page 24 for the answer.

3

2

1

Ant antics

Most animals leave ants alone because they bite and sting. Some kinds of spider look and behave like ants to fool their enemies.

Ants

The spider holds up two of its eight legs so it appears to have only six legs, like an ant.

The spider's upright front legs look like an ant's feelers.

Getting closer

The cleaner fish helps bigger fish by cleaning unwanted dirt and lice from their skin.

Cleaner fish

The sabre-toothed blenny looks like a cleaner fish, but it is really a hunter that tricks other fish.

Sabre-toothed blenny

Big fish let the blenny come near because they think it is a cleaner fish. But the blenny attacks them and takes bites out of their fins.

Whose egg?

Can you tell which of these eggs does not belong?

Reed warbler

The middle one is a cuckoo's egg. The rest belong to the reed warbler.

The cuckoo lays its egg in a reed warbler's nest. It is the same colour as the eggs that are already there. The warblers think the cuckoo's egg is their own so they look after it.

Signals

Some kinds of animals use colours and patterns as signals to each other.

Danger

A rabbit has a short, fluffy white tail. If it sees an enemy such as a fox, it runs quickly back to its burrow, flashing its tail in the air.

The white tail is a signal to other rabbits. It says "danger!".

Follow my leader

Ring-tailed lemurs are animals with long black and white tails. When a group of lemurs is on the move, they hold their tails up like flags.

Lemurs' tails help them to see each other and stay together. They are signals that say "follow me".

Getting angry

A tiger has bold, white spots on its ears. If one tiger is angry with another, it turns the backs of its ears forwards to show the white spots.

The white spots are a signal that warns other tigers to keep away.

Looking different

Colours can make it easier to tell similar animals apart. This helps animals to recognize others of their own kind.

Goldfinch

Chaffinch

These are the wings of two different finches. Their shape and size are the same, but the patterns and colours help to tell them apart.

People's colours

People also use colours to tell each other apart. All sports teams wear their own colours. This stops them getting mixed up with each other.

Different soccer teams wear different colours.

Being fed

Baby birds in nests wait for their parents to bring food. The babies' mouths are brightly coloured inside.

These baby great tits have bright orange mouths.

When a parent arrives with food, the babies open their mouths wide to show the colour inside. This is a signal to the parent. It says "feed me!".

Mysterious lights

Hatchet fish live deep at the bottom of the sea, where it is very dark. They have small patches on their bodies that light up and flash on and off.

Scientists think these lights could be signals to help hatchet fish recognize each other.

17

Showing off

Many male animals have bright colours to make them look attractive to females. This helps to bring the male and female together to breed.

Bright or brown

Male and female birds often look different from each other.

A male golden pheasant has beautifully coloured feathers which he shows off to attract a female.

The female pheasant has much duller colours. This helps her to hide when she is protecting her eggs and chicks.

18

Risky colours

Bright colours can also attract enemies. In spring a male paradise whydah's bright colours are easy to spot, and his long tail makes it hard for him to fly away.

After the whydah has found a female he loses his colours and long tail. For the rest of the year he stays plain brown.

Putting on a show

Some male birds put on a show to attract females. Every spring, male ruffs gather together. They puff up their feathers and fight. Females choose the males that put on the best show.

Three different male ruffs fighting

Colourful lizards

A male anolis lizard has an orange flap of skin under his throat. Usually it is folded up. But sometimes the lizard puffs it out and nods his head to show off the colour.

The bright throat attracts females. It also warns other males to keep out of the area.

Fierce faces

Mandrills are African monkeys. A male mandrill has a colourful face that gets brighter when he is looking for a female. The biggest and fiercest males are brightest of all.

A female mandrill chooses the male with the brightest colours. Other males keep away from him.

Collecting colours

A male bowerbird attracts a female by building a pile of twigs called a bower. He then decorates it with shells, flowers and bright, shiny things.

A female bowerbird chooses the male with the best bower. She then builds a nest and lays the eggs.

For a link to a bowerbird-matching game, go to www.usborne-quicklinks.com

Making colours

Fur, feathers, scales and skins can be all sorts of colours. Animals get these colours in many different ways.

Colours from food

Flamingos' feathers are pink because of a colouring called carotene which is found on water plants. Flamingos get carotene by eating tiny water animals that feed on these plants.

Often flamingos in zoos are not as pink as wild ones, because there is not enough carotene in their food.

Shiny colours

Many birds, such as sunbirds, have bright, shiny feathers. These change colour when lights falls on them from different directions.

This sunbird's feathers change from blue to green as the light shines on them.

Killed for colours

Some snakes are becoming rarer because people kill them for their beautiful skins.

This bag is made from the skin of a python.

Growing green

Animals do not normally grow green fur. But this sloth looks green. This is because tiny green plants called algae grow in its fur.

Black fur

Animals have a kind of colouring in their bodies called melanin. Melanin makes dark colours in fur and skin.

A black panther is really a leopard born with more melanin than usual. Its fur is black. But if you look closely you can still see the spots.

Jigsaw

Butterflies' patterns are made by thousands of tiny different-coloured scales that fit together.

Peacock butterfly scales

This is how the wing of a peacock butterfly looks close up. Can you see how the scales are arranged in rows?

White all over

Some animals are born white. They have no melanin so they cannot make dark colours. These are called albino animals.

An albino blackbird has white feathers.

Changes

Some animals can change their colours. Chameleons are lizards that change the colour of their skin to match different backgrounds.

This chameleon has a green pattern when it is hiding among leaves.

On sandy ground the same chameleon turns brown. It is always very hard to spot.

Sole survivor

The sole is a flatfish. It hides from enemies by lying flat on the sea bed. Its colour depends on where it lies.

This sole is the colour and pattern of the pebbles on which it is lying. If it moves onto mud, it becomes a muddy colour.

Sudden changes

If an octopus is in danger, different colours flash over its body. This surprises enemies and gives the octopus time to escape.

Colours also show how an octopus feels. For example, an angry octopus often turns red.

Internet links

For links to more websites about wildlife, go to the Usborne Quicklinks Website at **www.usborne-quicklinks.com** and click on the number of the website you want to visit.

Website 1 – Go on a virtual safari and see if you can identify some endangered animals.

Website 2 – Lots of facts and information about different types of mammals.

Website 3 – Find out more about chameleons and how they can change their skin colour then try an online game.

Website 4 – Imagine that you are a zookeeper preparing to look after a six-year-old Siberian tiger. You need to build it a home and choose the right food to make sure it thrives in your zoo.

Website 5 – Watch lots of different video clips of creatures living at a zoo, from baby animals to butterflies.

Website 6 – Lots of information about different types of habitats, including deserts and rainforests, with profiles of animals that live in them.

Website 7 – Why does a zebra have stripes? Find out by trying an online activity.

Website 8 – Click on the name of the underwater creature hiding in each picture then watch a video clip.

Index

Insect answers
Page 14 – None of the insects
in the picture is really a wasp.
Number 1 is a fly, number 2 is
a beetle, and number 3 is a
moth. You can see a real wasp
on page 12.

First published in 2001 by Usborne Publishing Ltd., Usborne House, 83-85 Saffron Hill, London EC1N 8RT, England. **www.usborne.com**
Copyright © 2001, 1992 Usborne Publishing Ltd. The name Usborne and the devices ♀ ⚭ are Trade Marks of Usborne Publishing
Ltd. All rights reserved. No part of this publication may be reproduced, stored in a retrieval system, or transmitted in any form or by
any means, electronic, mechanical, photocopying, recording, or otherwise, without the prior permission of the publisher.
Printed in China.